The 10 Commandments

God's Will be Done on Earth as it is in Heaven

Karen M. Matthews

ISBN: 0692554688
ISBN-13: 978-0692554685

DEDICATION

To sinners, may they find peace in the Mercy of God.

No one who conceals transgressions will prosper, but one who confesses and forsakes them will obtain mercy. Proverbs 28:13

CONTENTS

INTRODUCTION

Since the fall of man in the Garden of Eden, mankind has fought the tendency to sin and rebel against his Creator. The first human family demonstrated how far that fall had taken them in such a short time since the expulsion from the Garden of Eden when Cain killed his brother Abel in a jealous rage. Fortunately, God, our Father didn't turn his back on us, and in due time, gave Moses on Mount Sinai, the 10 commandments on tablets of stone to help us restore our relationship with both God and our fellow humans.

The commandments are God's rules that enable us to realize our duty as creatures, to be grateful to our Creator, and to show Him the proper respect and honor that He so deserves. They are also guideposts to help us live in true harmony with our fellow human beings, respecting each other in a community of authentic justice towards one another.

Throughout history, God revealed and reminded humankind of the justice of the 10 commandments, first to the Jews, then to the Gentiles who became Christ's followers; and later the followers of Mohamed also adopted them, such that these three monotheistic religions accepted the 10 commandments as the foundation for justice in their societies.

Unfortunately, modern man has become so ignorant of, or disdainful of, the 10 commandments that he assumes they are antiquated precepts that do not apply to humans in the present age. However, these sentiments could not be further from the truth.

The Jews know that the covenant that God made with them by giving His laws to Moses on Mt Sinai is an eternal covenant and will remain in force for all time.

> *I am the Lord, I have called you in righteousness, I have taken you by the hand and kept you; I have given you as a covenant to the people, a light to the nations, Isaiah 42:6*

When Jesus came, He told his followers that He did not come to abolish the 10 commandments and that they were still in effect with these words:

> *"Do not think that I have come to abolish the law or the prophets; I have come not to abolish but to fulfill. For truly I tell you, until heaven and earth pass away, not one letter, not one stroke of a letter, will pass from the law until all is accomplished." Matthew 5:17-18*

In fact, when someone asked Jesus what a person should do to obtain eternal life, he started rattling off the commandments:

> *Then someone came to him and said, "Teacher, what good deed must I do to have eternal life?" And he said to him, "Why do you ask me about what is good? There is only one who is good. If you wish to enter into life, keep the commandments." He said to him, "Which ones?" And Jesus said, "You shall not murder; You shall not commit adultery; You shall not steal; You shall not bear false witness; Honor your father and mother; also, You shall love your neighbor as yourself." Matthew 19:16-19*

So those preachers who preach that the 10 commandments are no longer binding on Christians or Jews or anyone else are sadly mistaken. Christ did not die to give his followers a "sinning license," but to reconcile mankind to the Father. In fact, Jesus said if we love him, we will keep his commandments.

> *"If you love me, you will keep my commandments. And I will ask the Father, and he will give you another Advocate, to be with you forever." John 14:15-16*

And those followers of Mohamed who distort the commandments to give them an excuse to be harsh or cruel towards others, are doing so at their own peril. If all of us, Jew, Christian, Muslim, or followers of another faith, would but follow the 10 commandments, we would respect each other and live in peace.

*Cursed is everyone who does not continue to do
everything written in the Book of the Law.
Galatians 3:10*

How to Use this Booklet

This booklet is designed to help the reader discern as an individual when he or she is breaking one of the 10 commandments. This is accomplished by first listing the text of the commandment (taken from the Old Testament) at the beginning of each chapter, followed by a list of sins that violate that commandment. The list is meant to be a complete and comprehensive list of sins that violates the commandment, although, through our human frailty, we may have inadvertently missed some of them.

The primary sources of the list of sins for each commandment are the Catechism of the Catholic Church and the Bible. Scripture verses are included to provide biblical evidence that a sin in the list is truly offensive to God, in case that we should doubt.

This list is meant to help us realize when we have failed to live up to God's law, so that we can ask for forgiveness. It should not be a cause for despair. What puts our souls in danger is not acknowledging our sinfulness and not asking for forgiveness.

*To the Lord our God belong mercy and forgiveness, for
we have rebelled against him. Daniel 9:9*

*If we confess our sins, he who is faithful and just will
forgive us our sins and cleanse us from all
unrighteousness. 1 John 1:9*

This list of sins also includes what St John calls sins unto death or mortal sin, depending on the translation of the Bible used.

*And this is the boldness we have in him, that if we
ask anything according to his will, he hears us. And if
we know that he hears us in whatever we ask, we
know that we have obtained the requests made of him.
If you see your brother or sister committing what is not
a mortal sin, you will ask, and God will give life to
such a one—to those whose sin is not mortal. There is*

*sin that is mortal; I do not say that you should pray
about that. All wrongdoing is sin, but there is sin that
is not mortal. 1 John 5:14-17*

Mortal sins break our relationship with God, kill the soul, and keep
us from heaven. When we commit a mortal sin, it is a serious
offense, requiring us to confess the sin to God and seek His
forgiveness, so that we can repair our relationship with God and
restore His grace in our souls. For Catholics, confession of the
mortal sin to a priest in the Sacrament of Reconciliation is the
proper way to restore our relationship to God. St Paul listed these
mortal sins in his letter to the Corinthians:

*Do you not know that wrongdoers will not inherit the
kingdom of God? Do not be deceived! Fornicators,
idolaters, adulterers, male prostitutes, sodomites,
thieves, the greedy, drunkards, revilers, robbers—none
of these will inherit the kingdom of God. And this is
what some of you used to be. But you were washed, you
were sanctified, you were justified in the name of the
Lord Jesus Christ and in the Spirit of our God.
1 Corinthians 6:9-11.*

On the other hand, venial sins are lesser sins, for example, petty
theft or telling a white lie, that do not completely break the
relationship with God, although they damage it and weaken our
will. For Catholics, praying the penitential rite at Mass, is an
excellent way to ask for forgiveness of venial sins. No matter what
your faith tradition, confessing your sins on a daily basis is a good
habit to develop to cleanse your soul and relieve your conscience.

Whether Jew, Christian, or Muslim, forgiveness starts with a
sincere feeling of remorse and a desire to seek God's pardon and
amend our ways. What happens next depends on your faith
tradition.

In the back of the booklet are prayers from each of these faith
traditions to aid the penitent in taking the first steps towards
reconciling with God. If you are a Jew, you would recite the
Tachanun (daily supplications) as well as confess your sins on the
Day of Atonement, Yom Kippur. If you are a Catholic, you will go
to the Sacrament of Reconciliation (also known as Confession) and

seek absolution by telling your sins to a priest and reciting the Act of Contrition prayer. If you are a Protestant Christian, you would pray the sinner's prayer, or similar prayer. If you are a Muslim, you would recite the Du'a (act of supplication).

Let the commandments be the safety net that keeps us out of hell and the narrow path that the Lord asks us to walk into eternal life.

"Enter through the narrow gate; for the gate is wide and the road is easy that leads to destruction, and there are many who take it. For the gate is narrow and the road is hard that leads to life, and there are few who find it." Matthew 7:13-14

Note: The numbering of the commandments presented in this booklet follow the Catholic tradition of St Augustine (354 – 430). Depending on your faith tradition, the numbering of the 10 commandments may be slightly different. For more information, read the "Ten Commandments" article on Wikipedia.

Sources: The Bible verses in this booklet come from the New Revised Standard Version Catholic Edition (NRSVCE), copyright © 1989, 1993 the Division of Christian Education of the National Council of the Churches of Christ in the United States of America.

The basis for the list of sins in this booklet comes primarily from the Catechism of the Catholic Church, Second Edition, revised in accordance with the official Latin text promulgated by Saint Pope John Paul II, English translation copyright © 1994, 1997, Section Two, The Ten Commandments 2083-2557.

Restore us, O God; let your face shine, that we may be saved. Psalm 80:30

THE FIRST COMMANDMENT

**You shall worship the Lord your God
and Him only shall you serve.
You shall have no other gods before Me. You shall
not make for yourself a graven image.**

Sins against this first commandment include:

Agnosticism – while neither rejecting nor affirming the existence of God, possessing an indifference to God's relevance or participation in the life of man.

> *Fools think their own way is right, but the wise listen to advice. Proverbs 12:15*

> *Where is the one who is wise? Where is the scribe? Where is the debater of this age? Has not God made foolish the wisdom of the world? 1 Corinthians 1:20*

> *Therefore I tell you, do not worry about your life, what you will eat or what you will drink, or about your body, or what you will wear. Is not life more than food, and the body more than clothing? Look at the birds of the air; they neither sow nor reap nor gather into barns, and yet your heavenly Father feeds them. Are you not of more value than they? Matthew 6:25-26*

Apostasy – the falling away from the Christian faith.

> *Now the Spirit expressly says that in later times some will renounce the faith by paying attention to deceitful spirits and teachings of demons, through the hypocrisy of liars whose consciences are seared with a hot iron. They forbid marriage and demand abstinence from foods, which God created to be received with*

thanksgiving by those who believe and know the truth.
1 Timothy 4:1-3

Atheism – a rejection or denial in the existence of God. A false sense that man is an end to himself.

> *Fools say in their hearts, "There is no God." They*
> *are corrupt, they commit abominable acts; there is no*
> *one who does good. Psalm 53:1*

> *For the doubter, being double-minded and unstable in*
> *every way, must not expect to receive anything from the*
> *Lord. James 1:7-8*

> *For certain intruders have stolen in among you, people*
> *who long ago were designated for this condemnation as*
> *ungodly, who pervert the grace of our God into*
> *licentiousness and deny our only Master and Lord,*
> *Jesus Christ. Jude 1:4*

Breaking a promise or vow to God – not adhering to or following through on a deliberate and free promise made to God, for example, marriage vows, or vows of chastity, poverty, and obedience by a religious (nun or monk).

> *If you make a vow to the Lord your God, do not*
> *postpone fulfilling it; for the Lord your God will surely*
> *require it of you, and you would incur guilt. But if*
> *you refrain from vowing, you will not incur guilt.*
> *Whatever your lips utter you must diligently perform,*
> *just as you have freely vowed to the Lord your God*
> *with your own mouth. Deuteronomy 23:21-23*

Despair – when man ceases to hope for his personal salvation from God, for help in attaining it or for the forgiveness of his sins. The Catechism of the Catholic Church states: "Despair is contrary to God's goodness, to his justice—for the Lord is faithful to his promises—and to his mercy." The mental state of depression is a mitigating factor for the culpability of this sin. God's mercy knows no bounds and He's the one who can truly read a person's heart.

But if we hope for what we do not see, we wait for it with patience. Romans 8:25

But we do not want you to be uninformed, brothers and sisters, about those who have died, so that you may not grieve as others do who have no hope. For since we believe that Jesus died and rose again, even so, through Jesus, God will bring with Him those who have died. 1 Thessalonians 4:13-14

Divination – the practice of seeking knowledge of the future or the unknown by supernatural means. All forms of divination are to be rejected, including conjuring up the dead, consulting horoscopes, astrology, palm reading, interpretation of omens and lots, use of mediums to contact the dead, and so forth. The Catechism of the Catholic Church states: "These practices contradict the honor, respect, and loving fear that we owe to God alone."

No one shall be found among you who makes a son or daughter pass through fire, or who practices divination, or is a soothsayer, or an augur, or a sorcerer, Deuteronomy 18:10

Hatred of God – comes from pride. It is contrary to love of God, whose goodness it denies, and whom it presumes to curse as the one who forbids sins and inflicts punishments.

So they reward me evil for good, and hatred for my love. Psalm 109:5

Heresy – false teaching; the obstinate post-baptismal denial of some truth which must be believed with divine and Catholic faith.

But false prophets also arose among the people, just as there will be false teachers among you, who will secretly bring in destructive opinions. They will even deny the Master who bought them—bringing swift destruction on themselves. Even so, many will follow their licentious ways, and because of these teachers the way of truth will be maligned. 1 Peter 2-1-2

But even if we or an angel from heaven should proclaim to you a gospel contrary to what we proclaimed to you, let that one be accursed! As we have said before, so now I repeat, if anyone proclaims to you a gospel contrary to what you received, let that one be accursed! Galatians 1:8-9

Hypocrisy – when one's own behavior does not conform to the moral standards that one claims to profess.

You hypocrite, first take the log out of your own eye, and then you will see clearly to take the speck out of your neighbor's eye. Matthew 7:5

Idolatry – giving one's worship, veneration, pre-eminent love to someone or something other than the one true God. Idolatry includes worship of Satan and false gods (polytheism), and putting love of activities (work, sports), persons (family, friends, and celebrities) and things (money, material goods) above our love for God. Jesus says, "You cannot serve God and mammon."

The Lord said to Moses, "Go down at once! Your people, whom you brought up out of the land of Egypt, have acted perversely; they have been quick to turn aside from the way that I commanded them; they have cast for themselves an image of a calf, and have worshiped it and sacrificed to it," Genesis 32:7-8

"No one can serve two masters; for a slave will either hate the one and love the other, or be devoted to the one and despise the other. You cannot serve God and wealth." Matthew 6:24

And the beast was captured, and with it the false prophet who had performed in its presence the signs by which he deceived those who had received the mark of the beast and those who worshiped its image. These two were thrown alive into the lake of fire that burns with sulfur. Revelation 19:20

Incredulity – the neglect of revealed truth or the willful refusal to assent to it.

> *He said to him, "If they do not listen to Moses and the prophets, neither will they be convinced, even if someone rises from the dead."* Luke 16:31

Ingratitude – thanklessness; a failure or refusal to acknowledge God's love and to love Him in return.

> *Enter His gates with thanksgiving, and His courts with praise. Give thanks to Him, bless His name. Psalm 100:4*

Involuntary doubt – a hesitation to believe and difficulty in overcoming objections connected with the faith, which can lead to spiritual blindness.

> *Now I desire to remind you, though you are fully informed, that the Lord, who once for all saved[a] a people out of the land of Egypt, afterward destroyed those who did not believe. Jude 1:5*

Lukewarmness – (also known as indifference) a hesitation or negligence to respond to God's love; a refusal to give oneself over to the prompting of charity.

> *So, because you are lukewarm, and neither cold nor hot, I am about to spit you out of my mouth. Revelations 3:16*

Magic, witchcraft, or sorcery – an attempt to use occult powers (intervention of demons) at one's service and exert them over others, whether the intentions behind them are good (to heal someone) or for bad (to harm others). This includes wearing charms or other practices that invoke evil powers.

> *…You shall not practice augury or witchcraft. Leviticus 19:26*

Not giving – not extending the love of God to others. If we are God's servants, we must spread His love to others by our actions.

*In all this I have given you an example that by such
work we must support the weak, remembering the
words of the Lord Jesus, for he himself said, 'It is
more blessed to give than to receive.'" Acts 20:35*

*How does God's love abide in anyone who has the
world's goods and sees a brother or sister in need and
yet refuses to help? 1 John 3:17*

Not praying – not communicating with God on a daily basis.

*Rejoice always, pray without ceasing, give thanks in
all circumstances; for this is the will of God in Christ
Jesus for you. 1 Thessalonians 5:16-18*

Not tithing – not giving back to God ten percent of our earnings.

*Will anyone rob God? Yet you are robbing me! But
you say, "How are we robbing you?" In your tithes
and offerings! You are cursed with a curse, for you are
robbing me—the whole nation of you! Bring the full
tithe into the storehouse, so that there may be food in
my house, and thus put me to the test, says the Lord of
hosts; see if I will not open the windows of heaven for
you and pour down for you an overflowing blessing.
Malachi 3:8-10*

Presumption – either a supposition upon man's own ability to save himself without help from God, or a supposition that God's almighty power or mercy saves a person without the person cooperating with God's grace and believing in and serving Him.

*"Not everyone who says to me, 'Lord, Lord,' will
enter the kingdom of heaven, but only the one who does
the will of my Father in heaven." Matthew 7:21*

Pride – a high or inordinate opinion of one's own dignity, importance, merit, or superiority, whether as cherished in the mind or as displayed in one's conduct. Loving self above all else.

*Pride goes before destruction, and a haughty spirit
before a fall. Proverbs 16:18*

*All those who are arrogant are an abomination to the
Lord; be assured, they will not go unpunished.
Proverbs 16:5*

*But he gives all the more grace; therefore it says, "God
opposes the proud, but gives grace to the humble."
James 4:6*

Sacrilege – profaning or treating unworthily the sacraments and
other liturgical actions, as well as persons, things, or places
consecrated to God. According to the Catechism of the Catholic
Church, sacrilege is a grave sin especially when committed against
Jesus' true body and blood in Holy Communion.

*All who eat it shall be subject to punishment, because
they have profaned what is holy to the Lord; and any
such person shall be cut off from the people.
Leviticus 19:8*

*If anyone destroys God's temple, God will destroy that
person. For God's temple is holy, and you are that
temple. 1 Corinthians 3:17*

*Whoever, therefore, eats the bread or drinks the cup of
the Lord in an unworthy manner will be answerable
for the body and blood of the Lord.
1Corinthians 11:27*

Schism – the refusal to submit to the Pope in communion with
the members of the Church subject to him. This is a sin against
the unity of the Church.

*Now I appeal to you, brothers and sisters, by the
name of our Lord Jesus Christ, that all of you be in
agreement and that there be no divisions among you,
but that you be united in the same mind and the same
purpose. 1 Corinthians 1:10*

Selfishness – primarily concerned with one's own interests,
benefits, welfare, and without regard for others.

*Do nothing from selfish ambition or conceit, but in
humility regard others as better than yourselves.
Philippians 2:3*

Self-righteousness – a self-perception, especially an unfounded
one, that one is totally correct or morally superior.

*He also told this parable to some who trusted in
themselves that they were righteous and regarded others
with contempt: "Two men went up to the temple to
pray, one a Pharisee and the other a tax collector.
The Pharisee, standing by himself, was praying thus,
'God, I thank you that I am not like other people:
thieves, rogues, adulterers, or even like this tax
collector. I fast twice a week; I give a tenth of all my
income.' But the tax collector, standing far off, would
not even look up to heaven, but was beating his breast
and saying, 'God, be merciful to me, a sinner!' I tell
you, this man went down to his home justified rather
than the other; for all who exalt themselves will be
humbled, but all who humble themselves will be
exalted." Luke 18:9-14*

Simony – the buying or selling of spiritual things.

*Now when Simon saw that the Spirit was given
through the laying on of the apostles' hands, he offered
them money, saying, "Give me also this power so that
anyone on whom I lay my hands may receive the Holy
Spirit." But Peter said to him, "May your silver
perish with you, because you thought you could obtain
God's gift with money!" Acts 8:18-20*

Spiritual sloth – a lack of effort towards one's own spiritual well-
being or the spiritual well-being of others.

*The appetite of the lazy craves, and gets nothing, while
the appetite of the diligent is richly supplied.
Proverbs 13:4*

Superstition – attributing magical or spiritual powers to certain practices or objects separate and apart from God's power.

> *Have nothing to do with profane myths and old wives' tales. Train yourself in godliness, 1 Timothy 4:7*

Tempting God – putting God's goodness and almighty power to the test by word or deed. The Catechism of the Catholic Church states: "Thus Satan tried to induce Jesus to throw himself down from the Temple and, by this gesture, force God to act."

> *Jesus said to him, "Again it is written, 'Do not put the Lord your God to the test.' " Matthew 4:7*

Vanity – excessive pride in one's appearance, qualities, abilities, and achievements; any preoccupation with beauty, fashion, decorating, etc.

> *I saw all the deeds that are done under the sun; and see, all is vanity and a chasing after wind. Ecclesiastes 1:14*

Voluntary doubt – a disregard or refusal to hold as true what God has revealed and the Church proposes for belief.

> *Although he had performed so many signs in their presence, they did not believe in him. John 12:37*

Worship of graven images – the worship of images representing pagan gods or their human representatives, or demons, i.e., statues or images of Baal, Ganesha, Shiva, Devi, Vishnu, Surya, Buddha, Krishna, etc., is prohibited. This does not apply to the veneration (not worship) of images of Jesus and the saints as decided by the church's second general council at Nicea (787 AD), concluding that by Jesus becoming a man and thus visible to the human eye, that His image could thereby be represented in sacred art.

> *Do not turn to idols or make cast images for yourselves: I am the Lord your God. Leviticus 19:4*

THE SECOND COMMANDMENT

You shall not take the name of
the Lord your God in vain.

Sins against this commandment include:

Blasphemy – uttering against God—inwardly or outwardly—words of hatred, reproach, or defiance. Also trivializing God's name by making it part of an exclamation, i.e., "Jesus!", "Jesus Christ!", "My God!"

> *Therefore I tell you, people will be forgiven for every sin and blasphemy, but blasphemy against the Spirit will not be forgiven. Matthew 12:31*

> *They set their mouths against heaven, and their tongues range over the earth. Psalm 73:9*

> *But you have dishonored the poor. Is it not the rich who oppress you? Is it not they who drag you into court? Is it not they who blaspheme the excellent name that was invoked over you? James 2:6-7*

Cursing – using God's name to invoke malice or condemnation towards another, i.e., "God damn you!"

> *and (they) cursed the God of heaven because of their pains and sores, and they did not repent of their deeds. Revelation 16:11*

False Oaths – Taking an oath or swearing is to take God as witness to what one affirms. The Catechism of the Catholic Church states: "It is to invoke the divine truthfulness as a pledge of one's own truthfulness." If the person is truthful in giving testimony in court, for example, then he/she does not violate the commandment, but if he/she is untruthful (commits perjury), then he/she violates this commandment.

> *Again, you have heard that it was said to those of ancient times, 'You shall not swear falsely, but carry out the vows you have made to the Lord.' But I say to*

you, Do not swear at all, either by heaven, for it is the throne of God, or by the earth, for it is his footstool, or by Jerusalem, for it is the city of the great King. And do not swear by your head, for you cannot make one hair white or black. Let your word be 'Yes, Yes' or 'No, No'; anything more than this comes from the evil one. Matthew 5:33-38

THE THIRD COMMANDMENT

Remember to keep holy the Sabbath Day.

Sins against this commandment include:

Failing to Worship God on His Day – not attending a worship service with the community of believers.

> *Jesus answered him, "It is written, Worship the Lord your God, and serve only him." Luke 4:8*

> *And let us consider how to provoke one another to love and good deeds, not neglecting to meet together, as is the habit of some, but encouraging one another, and all the more as you see the Day approaching. Hebrews 10:24-25*

> *"For where two or three gather in my name, there am I with them." Matthew 18:20*

> *Through him, then, let us continually offer a sacrifice of praise to God, that is, the fruit of lips that confess his name. Hebrews 13:15*

> *Like living stones, let yourselves be built into a spiritual house, to be a holy priesthood, to offer spiritual sacrifices acceptable to God through Jesus Christ. 1 Peter 2:5*

> *If I am delayed, you may know how one ought to behave in the household of God, which is the church of the living God, the pillar and bulwark of the truth. 1 Timothy 3:15*

Working on the Lord's Day – God set aside His day for humankind to refresh themselves, spending time with Him and their families. Doing unnecessary work is a sin against this commandment. One can argue that shopping on the Lord's Day, which causes others to work on this day is also sinful.

*But the seventh day is a Sabbath to the Lord your
God; you shall not do any work—you, your son or
your daughter, your male or female slave, your
livestock, or the alien resident in your towns.*
Exodus 20:10

Note: Jews keep Sabbath on Saturday, the historical observance of
the Sabbath. Most Christians observe the Lord's day on Sunday,
because Jesus rose from the dead on Sunday and the early
Christians celebrated the Lord Supper on the first day of the week
(Sunday) as indicated in the following scripture.

*On the first day of the week we came together to break
bread. Paul spoke to the people and, because he
intended to leave the next day, kept on talking until
midnight. Acts 20:7*

Christian denominations such as Seventh Day Baptists, Seventh
Day Adventists, and Church of God celebrate the Sabbath on
Saturday.

For Muslims, Friday is the official day of worship as taught by
Mohammed and stated in the Quran:

*O you who believe! When the call to prayer is
proclaimed on Friday hasten earnestly to the
remembrance of God, and leave aside business. That
is best for you if you but knew. Quran 62:9*

THE FOURTH COMMANDMENT

Honor your father and mother.

Sins against this commandment include:

Bad parenting – not honoring your role as a mother and father and not providing for, nurturing, and educating your children both physically and spiritually. For Catholics, failure to baptize your children in a reasonable time after birth (and accept God's free gift of salvation for your child), would be sinful, because it denies children the grace God desires to give them for proper training in the spiritual life. Mary and Joseph were dutiful in taking Jesus to the temple at the appointed time as directed by Jewish law.

> *When the time came for their purification according to the law of Moses, they brought him up to Jerusalem to present him to the Lord (as it is written in the law of the Lord, "Every firstborn male shall be designated as holy to the Lord"), Luke 2:22-23*

Some Christian denominations baptize babies in infancy and others dedicate their children in their houses of worship, similar to how Jesus was presented in the temple according to Jewish tradition. Most important is to raise your children in the ways of the Lord.

> *Recite them (the commandments) to your children and talk about them when you are at home and when you are away, when you lie down and when you rise. Deuteronomy 6:7*

> *And, fathers, do not provoke your children to anger, but bring them up in the discipline and instruction of the Lord. Ephesians 6:4*

Disobedience – not obeying your parents when you are young or dismissing their advice when you are an adult.

Disrespect – not treating your parents with respect in this life and after they are deceased. For example, failing to carry out the wishes in your parents' Last Will and Testament would be sinful.

Neglect – not spending time with your parents and showing them love and affection. Not caring for them in their old age. Think twice before putting your parents in a nursing home if you are able to care for them yourself.

> *Children, obey your parents in the Lord, for this is right. "Honor your father and mother"—which is the first commandment with a promise—"so that it may go well with you and that you may enjoy long life on the earth." Ephesians 6:1-3*

THE FIFTH COMMANDMENT

You shall not kill.

Abortion – killing a child in the womb (from the moment of conception); this includes the use of in vitro fertilization that allows some fertilized eggs to be destroyed, and the taking of drugs (abortifacients) such as the morning after pill. Even birth control pills may allow a woman to conceive, but cause a woman's body to be hostile to the embryo such that it is expelled from the womb, causing its death; therefore, taking birth control pills should be avoided. Voting for politicians whose policies promote abortion is also a sin.

> *"Before I formed you in the womb I knew you, and before you were born I consecrated you; I appointed you a prophet to the nations." Jeremiah 1:5*

> *For it was you who formed my inward parts; you knit me together in my mother's womb. I praise you, for I am fearfully and wonderfully made. Wonderful are your works; that I know very well. My frame was not hidden from you, when I was being made in secret, intricately woven in the depths of the earth. Your eyes beheld my unformed substance. In your book were written all the days that were formed for me, when none of them as yet existed. Psalm 39: 13-16*

> *Thus says the Lord: For three transgressions of the Ammonites, and for four, I will not revoke the punishment; because they have ripped open pregnant women in Gilead in order to enlarge their territory. Amos 1:13*

> *I call heaven and earth to witness against you today that I have set before you life and death, blessings and curses. Choose life so that you and your descendants may live. Deuteronomy 30:19*

Abuse (verbal or emotional) – uttering unkind words or treating people in such a way as to damage a person's self-esteem.

> *When the righteous cry for help, the Lord hears, and rescues them from all their troubles. The Lord is near to the brokenhearted, and saves the crushed in spirit. Many are the afflictions of the righteous, but the Lord rescues them from them all. He keeps all their bones; not one of them will be broken. Psalm 34:17-20*

Abuse of alcohol, drugs, or food – killing ourselves slowly by using illicit drugs or overindulging in food or drink to the detriment of our bodies.

> *Do not get drunk with wine, for that is debauchery; but be filled with the Spirit. Ephesians 5:18*

> *Wine is a mocker, strong drink a brawler, and whoever is led astray by it is not wise. Proverbs 20:1*

Anger – a hostile emotional response to someone else's action or perceived action. Provoking someone to anger is also sinful.

> *You must understand this, my beloved: let everyone be quick to listen, slow to speak, slow to anger; for your anger does not produce God's righteousness. James 1:19-20*

> *Do not be quick to anger, for anger lodges in the bosom of fools. Ecclesiastes 7:9*

> *A soft answer turns away wrath, but a harsh word stirs up anger. Proverbs 15:1*

Animal cruelty – harming or neglecting animals or killing them for no good reason, for example, not for food.

> *The righteous know the needs of their animals, but the mercy of the wicked is cruel. Proverbs 12:10*

Disrespect for the dead – not showing respect for the dead by not providing a proper burial (or cremation). We should honor the children of God, who are temples of the Holy Spirit, and any deceased person as a person made in the image of God.

*Now while Jesus was at Bethany in the house of
Simon the leper, a woman came to him with an
alabaster jar of very costly ointment, and she poured it
on his head as he sat at the table. But when the
disciples saw it, they were angry and said, "Why this
waste? For this ointment could have been sold for a
large sum, and the money given to the poor." But
Jesus, aware of this, said to them, "Why do you
trouble the woman? She has performed a good service
for me. For you always have the poor with you, but
you will not always have me. By pouring this ointment
on my body she has prepared me for burial. Truly I
tell you, wherever this good news is proclaimed in the
whole world, what she has done will be told in
remembrance of her." Matthew 26:6-13*

Euthanasia – a deliberate act of killing someone who is very sick
or injured in order to prevent any more suffering. The Catechism
of the Catholic Church states "Discontinuing medical procedures
that are burdensome, dangerous, extraordinary, or disproportionate
to the expected outcome can be legitimate." In other words, it
allows the natural course of death to take place and does not
constitute euthanasia. However, basic care of food and water that
all humans need to live should not be withheld.

*For your own lifeblood I will surely require a
reckoning: from every animal I will require it and from
human beings, each one for the blood of another, I will
require a reckoning for human life. Whoever sheds the
blood of a human, by a human shall that person's
blood be shed; for in His own image God made
humankind. Genesis 9:5-6*

Fighting or arguing – causing conflicts and arguments, especially
when not aimed at resolving problems.

*But avoid stupid controversies, genealogies, dissensions,
and quarrels about the law, for they are unprofitable
and worthless. After a first and second admonition,
have nothing more to do with anyone who causes*

*divisions, since you know that such a person is
perverted and sinful, being self-condemned.
Titus 3:9-11*

*It is honorable to refrain from strife, but every fool is
quick to quarrel. Proverbs 20:3*

Fratricide – killing a brother or sister.

Gloating – taking pleasure in another person's suffering.

*Do not rejoice when your enemies fall, and do not let
your heart be glad when they stumble, or else the Lord
will see it and be displeased, and turn away his anger
from them. Proverbs 24:17-18*

Gluttony – overeating. Also see abuse of alcohol, drugs, or food.

*Do not be among winebibbers, or among gluttonous
eaters of meat; for the drunkard and the glutton will
come to poverty, and drowsiness will clothe them with
rags. Proverbs 23:20-21*

Hatred – extreme dislike of another and desire that evil or harm
should come to that person.

*All who hate a brother or sister are murderers, and
you know that murderers do not have eternal life
abiding in them. 1 John 3:15*

*Hatred stirs up strife, but love covers all offenses.
Proverbs 10:12*

Indirect killing - exposing someone to mortal danger without
grave reason, as well as refusing to assist someone in danger. The
Catechism of the Catholic Church states, "The acceptance by
human society of murderous famines, without efforts to remedy
them, is a scandalous injustice and a grave offense. Those whose
usurious and avaricious dealings lead to the hunger and death of
their brethren in the human family indirectly commit homicide,
which is imputable to them."

How does God's love abide in anyone who has the world's goods and sees a brother or sister in need and yet refuses help? 1 John 3:17

Infanticide – killing an infant.

Kidnapping – taking someone hostage whether to perpetrate evil acts on them, ask for ransom, or for any reason.

Whoever kidnaps a person, whether that person has been sold or is still held in possession, shall be put to death. Exodus 21:16

Matricide – killing a spouse.

Murder – direct and intentional killing of another, a serious sin. Killing in self-defense, including when in combat is not murder, but all peaceful efforts should be made to avoid war and confrontation.

Blessed are the peacemakers, for they will be called children of God. Matthew 5:9

Mutilation of the Body - Except when performed for strictly therapeutic medical reasons, directly intended amputations, mutilations, and sterilizations performed on innocent persons are against the moral law (definition from the Catechism of the Catholic Church). Unnecessary cosmetic surgery and tattoos are also prohibited.

I appeal to you therefore, brothers and sisters,[a] by the mercies of God, to present your bodies as a living sacrifice, holy and acceptable to God, which is your spiritual worship. Romans 12:1

You shall not make any gashes in your flesh for the dead or tattoo any marks upon you: I am the Lord. Leviticus 19:28

Neglect of health – not taking the necessary steps to safeguard your own health and the health of others.

Before you speak, learn; and before you fall ill, take care of your health. Sirach 18:19

Do not be wise in your own eyes; fear the Lord, and turn away from evil. It will be a healing for your flesh and a refreshment for your body. Proverbs 3:8

Patricide – killing a parent.

Polluting the environment – The earth was created by God and the creatures, plants, animals, and materials in it give Him glory. God gave man dominion over the earth and we should not damage it.

Then God said, "Let us make humankind in our image, according to our likeness; and let them have dominion over the fish of the sea, and over the birds of the air, and over the cattle, and over all the wild animals of the earth, and over every creeping thing that creeps upon the earth." Genesis 1:26

The earth brought forth vegetation: plants yielding seed of every kind, and trees of every kind bearing fruit with the seed in it. And God saw that it was good. Genesis 1:12

The Lord God took the man and put him in the Garden of Eden to till it and keep it. Genesis 2:15

Rudeness – a display of disrespect by not complying with the social norms or etiquette of a group or culture.

Love is patient; love is kind; love is not envious or boastful or arrogant or rude. It does not insist on its own way; it is not irritable or resentful; it does not rejoice in wrongdoing, but rejoices in the truth. 1 Corinthians 13:4-6

But I say to you that if you are angry with a brother or sister, you will be liable to judgment; and if you insult a brother or sister, you will be liable to the council; and if you say, 'You fool,' you will be liable to the hell of fire. Matthew 5:22

Scandal – is an attitude or behavior that leads another to do evil as it may tempt our neighbor to engage in acts that kills his soul. Likewise, participating in another person's sin or helping another person to sin is sinful.

> *Jesus said to his disciples, "Occasions for stumbling are bound to come, but woe to anyone by whom they come! It would be better for you if a millstone were hung around your neck and you were thrown into the sea than for you to cause one of these little ones to stumble." Luke 17:1-2*

Sloth or laziness – lack of effort, refusal to work, a preoccupation with leisure; also see spiritual sloth under the first commandment. Sloth keeps a person from performing the necessary tasks to take care of one's self and family, killing one's livelihood. It also wounds the community because the person doesn't carry his/her share of the workload.

> *The appetite of the lazy craves, and gets nothing, while the appetite of the diligent is richly supplied. Proverbs 13:4*

Suicide – the killing of one's self and is the ultimate act of despair which is contrary to the hope in God's providence. Anyone who aids a person to commit suicide is also participating in the killing of that individual. The Catechism of the Catholic Church states: "Grave psychological disturbances, anguish, or grave fear of hardship, suffering, or torture can diminish the responsibility of the one committing suicide. We should not despair of the eternal salvation of persons who have taken their own lives. By ways known to him alone, God can provide the opportunity for salutary repentance. The Church prays for persons who have taken their own lives."

> *Do you not know that you are God's temple and that God's Spirit dwells in you? If anyone destroys God's temple, God will destroy that person. For God's temple is holy, and you are that temple. 1 Corinthians 3:16-17*

Terrorism – to threaten, wound, or kill to strike fear in others.

For I hear many whispering: "Terror is all around!
Denounce him! Let us denounce him!" All my close
friends are watching for me to stumble. "Perhaps he
can be enticed, and we can prevail against him, and
take our revenge on him." Jeremiah 20:10

For I hear the whispering of many—terror all
around!—as they scheme together against me, as they
plot to take my life. Psalm 31:13

Torture – the use of physical or moral violence to extract confessions, punish the guilty, frighten opponents, or satisfy hatred. According to the Catechism of the Catholic Church, torture is contrary to respect for the person and for human dignity. This includes torturing prisoners of war, no matter if the goal might be good, for example, to illicit information or a confession. Jesus suffered torture at the hands of Pilot's soldiers. Torture is something no one should have to suffer.

So he released Barabbas for them; and after flogging
Jesus, he handed him over to be crucified.
Matthew 27:26

THE SIXTH COMMANDMENT

You shall not commit adultery.

Sins against this commandment include:

Adultery – voluntary sexual intercourse between a married person and a person who is not his or her spouse. This also includes divorcing a spouse when the couple is married in a religious ceremony (what God has joined together let no one separate) and remarrying another (without having that marriage declared null by the Church). Entering a new union, even if it is recognized by civil law, puts remarried spouses in a situation of public and permanent adultery. For detailed information about the sins against marriage described in this section, refer to the Catechism of the Catholic Church, Section Two, The Ten Commandments, Article 6, The Sixth Commandment, 2331-2400.

> He answered, "Have you not read that the one who made them at the beginning 'made them male and female,' and said, 'For this reason a man shall leave his father and mother and be joined to his wife, and the two shall become one flesh'? So they are no longer two, but one flesh. Therefore what God has joined together, let no one separate." Matthew 19:4-6

Bestiality – sexual activity between humans and animals.

> You shall not have sexual relations with any animal and defile yourself with it, nor shall any woman give herself to an animal to have sexual relations with it: it is perversion. Leviticus 18:23

Contraception – methods or devices used to prevent pregnancy. Artificial contraception is sinful because it goes against God's plan for marriage. As soon as God created Adam and Eve, he blessed them and commanded them to have children.

> God blessed them, and God said to them, "Be fruitful and multiply, and fill the earth and subdue it; and have dominion over the fish of the sea and over the

*birds of the air and over every living thing that moves
upon the earth." Genesis 1:28*

God doesn't take this command away from married couples just
because there are billions of people on the earth or because
humans have created the condom and birth control pills. God
alone has dominion over the population of the world. God was so
upset at Onan's practice of birth control (coitus interruptus) in the
Book of Genesis that he put him to death. Onan was obligated
under Jewish law at the time to take his brother's wife as a wife
after his brother died.

*Then Judah said to Onan, "Go in to your brother's
wife and perform the duty of a brother-in-law to her;
raise up offspring for your brother." But since Onan
knew that the offspring would not be his, he spilled his
semen on the ground whenever he went in to his
brother's wife, so that he would not give offspring to his
brother. What he did was displeasing in the sight of
the Lord, and he put him to death also.
Genesis 38:8-10*

God gave us the natural rhythm of a woman's body to be fertile
only a few days a month. Abstaining from conjugal love during
these fertile times is not wrong, if there are serious physical or
mental health reasons, or financial hardships that would result from
bringing more children into the family. The idea that we as human
beings should plan our families instead of letting God plan them is
contrary to the spirit of the "Our Father" prayer that Jesus taught
us to pray: "Thy will be done on earth as it is in heaven."

Divorce – Divorce is a grave offense against the natural law as it
breaks the promise before God, to which the spouses freely
consented, to live with each other until death. Divorce breaks the
covenantal bond, injures the spouses, hurts the children, and
introduces disorder into the family and society.

*Some Pharisees came to him, and to test him they
asked, "Is it lawful for a man to divorce his wife for
any cause?" He answered, "Have you not read that
the one who made them at the beginning 'made them*

male and female,' and said, 'For this reason a man shall leave his father and mother and be joined to his wife, and the two shall become one flesh'? So they are no longer two, but one flesh. Therefore what God has joined together, let no one separate." They said to him, "Why then did Moses command us to give a certificate of dismissal and to divorce her?" He said to them, "It was because you were so hard-hearted that Moses allowed you to divorce your wives, but from the beginning it was not so. And I say to you, whoever divorces his wife, except for unchastity, and marries another commits adultery." Matthew 19:3-9

Fornication – sexual intercourse and other sexual acts between an unmarried man and an unmarried woman. The Catechism of the Catholic Church states: "It is gravely contrary to the dignity of persons and of human sexuality which is naturally ordered to the good of spouses and the generation and education of children. Moreover, it is a grave scandal when there is corruption of the young."

But fornication and impurity of any kind, or greed, must not even be mentioned among you, as is proper among saints. Ephesians 5:3

For this is the will of God, your sanctification: that you abstain from fornication; that each one of you know how to control your own body in holiness and honor, 1 Thessalonians 4:3-4

Homosexual acts – sexual relations between persons of the same sex, men with men, and women with women is a serious sin.

For this reason God gave them up to degrading passions. Their women exchanged natural intercourse for unnatural, and in the same way also the men, giving up natural intercourse with women, were consumed with passion for one another. Men committed shameless acts with men and received in

their own persons the due penalty for their error.
Romans 1:26-27

If a man lies with a male as with a woman, both of
them have committed an abomination.
Leviticus 20:13

The Catechism of the Catholic Church states: "Homosexual acts
are contrary to the natural law; they close the sexual act to the gift
of life and do not reflect God's plan for creation."

So God created humankind in his image, in the image
of God he created them; male and female he created
them. Genesis 1:27

He answered, "Have you not read that the one who
made them at the beginning 'made them male and
female,' and said, 'For this reason a man shall leave
his father and mother and be joined to his wife, and
the two shall become one flesh'? So they are no longer
two, but one flesh. Therefore what God has joined
together, let no one separate." Matthew 19:4-6

Same sex attraction is not sinful, but rather a temptation. Persons
with same sex attraction are called to chastity and can overcome
this sin with God's grace.

Jesus looked at them and said, "For mortals it is
impossible, but not for God; for God all things are
possible. Mark 10:27

Incest – sexual relations between people classified as being too
closely related to marry each other. The Catechism of the Catholic
Church states: "incest corrupts family relationships and marks a
regression toward animality."

It is actually reported that there is sexual immorality
among you, and of a kind that is not found even
among pagans; for a man is living with his father's
wife. 1 Corinthians 5:1

Masturbation – the sexual stimulation of one's own genitals for
sexual arousal or other sexual pleasure, usually to the point of

orgasm. The Catechism of the Catholic Church states: "The deliberate use of the sexual faculty, for whatever reason, outside of marriage is essentially contrary to its purpose. For here, sexual pleasure is sought outside of the sexual relationship, which is demanded by the moral order and in which the total meaning of mutual self-giving and human procreation in the context of true love is achieved."

> *Live by the Spirit, I say, and do not gratify the desires*
> *of the flesh. Galatians 5:16*

Pedophilia – sexual abuse of children and adolescents. Robbing children of their sexual innocence is a serious sin, especially when it is done by adults who are caregivers or authority figures.

> *"If any of you put a stumbling block before one of*
> *these little ones who believe in me, it would be better*
> *for you if a great millstone were fastened around your*
> *neck and you were drowned in the depth of the sea."*
> *Matthew 18:6*

Pornography – reading or viewing sexually explicit material (magazines, books, movies, plays, music, etc.). Viewing real-life sexual acts performed by others, also known as voyeurism, and viewing mainstream commercial movies with explicit sexual scenes, is also sinful. The Catechism of the Catholic Church states: "Removing real or simulated sexual acts from the intimacy of the partners, in order to display them deliberately to third parties…offends against chastity because it perverts the conjugal act, the intimate giving of spouses to each other. It does grave injury to the dignity of its participants (actors, vendors, the public), since each one becomes an object of base pleasure and illicit profit for others. It immerses all who are involved in the illusion of a fantasy world. It is a grave offense. Civil authorities should prevent the production and distribution of pornographic materials."

> *for all that is in the world—the desire of the flesh, the*
> *desire of the eyes, the pride in riches—comes not from*
> *the Father but from the world. 1 John 2:16*

Prostitution – the business or practice of engaging in sexual relations in exchange for payment or some other benefit. This includes "sugar daddy" and "gigolo" relationships in which a female or male receives upkeep and expensive gifts for engaging in a sexual relationship with a wealthy individual. The Catechism of the Catholic Church states "Prostitution does injury to the dignity of the person who engages in it, reducing the person to an instrument of sexual pleasure. The one who pays sins gravely against himself: he violates the chastity to which his Baptism pledged him and defiles his body, the temple of the Holy Spirit. Prostitution is a social scourge. It usually involves women, but also men, children, and adolescents (The latter two cases involve the added sin of scandal.). While it is always gravely sinful to engage in prostitution, the imputability of the offense can be attenuated by destitution, blackmail, or social pressure."

> *Do not profane your daughter by making her a*
> *prostitute, that the land not become prostituted and*
> *full of depravity. Leviticus 19:29*

Rape – the forcible violation of the sexual intimacy of another person. The Catechism of the Catholic Church states: "Rape deeply wounds the respect, freedom, and physical and moral integrity to which every person has a right. It causes grave damage that can mark the victim for life."

> *She answered him, "No, my brother, do not violate*
> *me, for such a thing is not done in Israel; do not do*
> *this outrageous thing. As for me, where could I carry*
> *my shame? And as for you, you would be as one of the*
> *outrageous fools in Israel. Now therefore, please speak*
> *to the king, for he will not withhold me from you."*
> *But he would not listen to her, and being stronger than*
> *she, he violated her and lay with her. 2 Samuel*
> *13:12-14*

Sodomy – anal sex, often associated with homosexual males, but can also be committed by heterosexual persons. St Paul mentions this sin as one that keeps us out of heaven.

> *Do you not know that wrongdoers will not inherit the*
> *kingdom of God? Do not be deceived! Fornicators,*
> *idolaters, adulterers, male prostitutes, sodomites,*
> *thieves, the greedy, drunkards, revilers, robbers—none*
> *of these will inherit the kingdom of God. And this is*
> *what some of you used to be. But you were washed, you*
> *were sanctified, you were justified in the name of the*
> *Lord Jesus Christ and in the Spirit of our God.*
> *1 Corinthians 6: 9-11.*

THE SEVENTH COMMANDMENT

You shall not steal.

Acquiring debts and failing to pay them – buying things we do not need and putting them on credit puts our financial well-being and that of our family in jeopardy and should be avoided, unless absolutely necessary. God's desire for our lives is to live within our means. Defaulting on one's debts is likewise sinful and should be avoided.

> *Pay to all what is due them—taxes to whom taxes*
> *are due, revenue to whom revenue is due, respect to*
> *whom respect is due, honor to whom honor is due.*
> *Romans 13:7*

Economic injustice – denying people access to work, creating an environment in society that puts profit over the livelihood of persons, is wrong. Citizens should support leaders who will create a positive economy that benefits individuals and the common good.

> *Do not rob the poor because they are poor, or crush the*
> *afflicted at the gate; for the Lord pleads their cause*
> *and despoils of life those who despoil them.*
> *Proverbs 22:22-23*

Gambling – playing at a game of chance for money or other stakes. The Catechism of the Catholic Church states: "Games of chance (card games, etc.) or wagers are not in themselves contrary to justice. They become morally unacceptable when they deprive someone of what is necessary to provide for his needs and those of others." For example, gambling away funds that are needed to pay the bills and buy food for the family deprives them of the care they need.

> *Wealth hastily gotten will dwindle, but those who*
> *gather little by little will increase it. Proverbs 13:11*

Neglecting to care for the disabled, elderly, poor, and disadvantaged in our society – Jesus said that what you do for the least of brothers, you do for Him. Jesus' parables about Lazarus and the rich man (Luke 16:19-25) and the last judgment (Matthew 25: 41-45) should send chills up our spines.

> *Those who despise their neighbors are sinners, but happy are those who are kind to the poor.*
> *Proverbs 14:21*

> *Then he will say to those at his left hand, 'You that are accursed, depart from me into the eternal fire prepared for the devil and his angels; for I was hungry and you gave me no food, I was thirsty and you gave me nothing to drink, I was a stranger and you did not welcome me, naked and you did not give me clothing, sick and in prison and you did not visit me.' Then they also will answer, 'Lord, when was it that we saw you hungry or thirsty or a stranger or naked or sick or in prison, and did not take care of you?' Then he will answer them, 'Truly I tell you, just as you did not do it to one of the least of these, you did not do it to me.'*
> *Matthew 25: 41-45*

Not doing an honest day's work – doing other things at work (goofing off, idle chatting with coworkers, browsing the internet) when we should be working for our employer is stealing time from the employer.

> *Thieves must give up stealing; rather let them labor and work honestly with their own hands, so as to have something to share with the needy. Ephesians 4:28*

Paying unfair wages – employers that do not pay a just wage to employees are stealing from them.

> *Now to one who works, wages are not reckoned as a gift but as something due. Romans 4:4*

Stealing – taking goods that belong to someone else. Stealing can be a minor sin like taking a piece of gum or a serious "mortal" sin like armed robbery. Serious sins should be confessed as soon as possible with a sincere heart of repentance. Repentance should include restitution (paying back what was stolen). Damaging someone else's goods is also sinful.

> *Treasures gained by wickedness do not profit, but*
> *righteousness delivers from death.* Proverbs 10:2

Usury – financial institutions or individuals who charge high interest for lending money are stealing from others.

> *If you lend money to my people, to the poor among you,*
> *you shall not deal with them as a creditor; you shall*
> *not exact interest from them.* Exodus 22:25

THE EIGHTH COMMANDMENT

You shall not bear false witness against your neighbor.

Bigotry – an obstinate, irrational, or unfair intolerance of ideas, opinions, or beliefs that differ from one's own, and intolerance of the people who hold them. This is a form of rash judgment.

> *There is no longer Jew or Greek, there is no longer slave or free, there is no longer male and female; for all of you are one in Christ Jesus. Galatians 3:28*

> *When they arrived, they called the church together and related all that God had done with them, and how he had opened a door of faith for the Gentiles. Acts 14:27*

> *And he died for all, so that those who live might live no longer for themselves, but for him who died and was raised for them. 2 Corinthians 5:15*

Boasting – prideful talk about one's own accomplishments, possessions or abilities.

> *Do not boast about tomorrow, for you do not know what a day may bring. Proverbs 27:1*

> *They pour out words, speaking arrogant things; all who do evil boast proudly. Psalm 94:4*

Deceit – concealing or misrepresenting the truth by actions as well as speech. Passing yourself off as the opposite sex to what you truly biologically are (for example, cross dressing) is an example of deceit.

> *A woman shall not wear a man's apparel, nor shall a man put on a woman's garment; for whoever does such things is abhorrent to the Lord your God. Deuteronomy 22:5*

You destroy those who speak lies; the Lord abhors the bloodthirsty and deceitful. Psalm 5:6

Detraction – disclosing someone's faults to another without a valid reason to do so.

Besides that, they learn to be idle, gadding about from house to house; and they are not merely idle, but also gossips and busybodies, saying what they should not say. 1 Timothy 5:13

Gossiping – telling derogatory information about someone, even if it is true, damages a person's reputation and is sinful.

A perverse person spreads strife, and a whisperer separates close friends. Proverbs 16:28

Judging Others – assuming, without sufficient evidence, the moral fault of another. This does not refer to discernment between good and evil as we are obliged to follow our consciences that are founded on God's laws.

"Do not judge, so that you may not be judged." Matthew 7:1

Lying – telling any untruth.

Lying lips are an abomination to the Lord, but those who act faithfully are his delight. Proverbs 12:22

Not defending God's truth in society – failing to speak up for God's truth when it is misrepresented or maligned.

"Those who are ashamed of me and of my words in this adulterous and sinful generation, of them the Son of Man will also be ashamed when he comes in the glory of his Father with the holy angels." Mark 8:38

"Everyone therefore who acknowledges me before others, I also will acknowledge before my Father in heaven; but whoever denies me before others, I also will deny before my Father in heaven." Matthew 10:32-33

Perjury – giving false testimony in court.

> *A false witness will not go unpunished, and the liar will perish. Proverbs 19:9*
>
> *Do not be a witness against your neighbor without cause, and do not deceive with your lips. Proverbs 24:28*

Slander – telling lies about another person kills that person's reputation.

> *Lying lips conceal hatred, and whoever utters slander is a fool. Proverbs 10:18*
>
> *One who secretly slanders a neighbor I will destroy. Psalm 101:5*
>
> *A haughty look and an arrogant heart I will not tolerate. Psalm 101:5*

Violating someone's privacy – betraying someone's confidence by communicating personal information about someone to someone else when there is no valid reason for doing so. For example, if someone confessed a crime, you would be justified in telling this to the authorities. Prying into someone's private matters without good reason would also be sinful.

> *Argue your case with your neighbor directly, and do not disclose another's secret; or else someone who hears you will bring shame upon you, and your ill repute will have no end. Proverbs 25:9-10*
>
> *Like somebody who takes a passing dog by the ears is one who meddles in the quarrel of another. Proverbs 26:17*

THE NINTH COMMANDMENT

You shall not covet your neighbor's wife

Coveting another's spouse – desiring, flirting with, or luring another person's spouse.

> *It happened, late one afternoon, when David rose from his couch and was walking about on the roof of the king's house, that he saw from the roof a woman bathing; the woman was very beautiful. David sent someone to inquire about the woman. It was reported, "This is Bathsheba daughter of Eliam, the wife of Uriah the Hittite." So David sent messengers to get her, and she came to him, and he lay with her.*
> *2 Samuel 11:2-4*

Immodesty – nakedness; exposing your body to others in an unchaste and improper way. People who dress immodestly tempt others to lust and bear some responsibility for their sin.

> *Also that the women should dress themselves modestly and decently in suitable clothing, not with their hair braided, or with gold, pearls, or expensive clothes, but with good works, as is proper for women who profess reverence for God. 1 Timothy 2:9-10*

Impure thoughts – entertaining thoughts of an unchaste sexual nature. Such thoughts might come into our minds as a temptation, but we should quickly dispel them through use of prayer.

> *For out of the heart come evil thoughts and plans, murders, adulteries, sexual immoralities, thefts, false testimonies, slanders (verbal abuse, irreverent speech, blaspheming). Matthew 15:19*

Licentiousness – lacking legal or moral restraints, especially as it pertains to sexual mores. This also includes supporting laws and civic leaders that foster a social environment of sexual immorality.

> *Now the works of the flesh are obvious: fornication, impurity, licentiousness, idolatry, sorcery, enmities, strife, jealousy, anger, quarrels, dissensions, factions, envy, drunkenness, carousing, and things like these. I am warning you, as I warned you before: those who do such things will not inherit the kingdom of God. Galatians 5:19-21*

Lust – disordered desire for or inordinate enjoyment of sexual pleasure. The Catechism of the Catholic Church states: "Sexual pleasure is morally disordered when sought for itself, isolated from its procreative and unitive purposes."

> *But I say to you that everyone who looks at a woman with lust has already committed adultery with her in his heart. Matthew 5:28*

Vulgar language – using obscene language such as the four letter "f" word for sexual intercourse is rooted in lust and contrary to the dignity of the human person who is made in the image of God; telling dirty jokes is also a violation of this commandment.

> *Then he called the crowd to him and said to them, "Listen and understand: it is not what goes into the mouth that defiles a person, but it is what comes out of the mouth that defiles." Matthew 15:10-12*

> *Entirely out of place is obscene, silly, and vulgar talk; but instead, let there be thanksgiving. Ephesians 5:4*

THE TENTH COMMANDMENT

You shall not covet your neighbor's goods

Avarice – insatiable greed for riches; inordinate, miserly desire to gain and hoard wealth.

> *The wicked covet the proceeds of wickedness, but the root of the righteous bears fruit. Proverbs 12:12*

Covetousness – having a craving for possessions. If you are consumed with wanting and shopping for material things, even if you can afford it, you are engaging in this sin. Think of what good you could be doing instead of accumulating earthly treasures.

> *Do not store up for yourselves treasures on earth, where moth and rust consume and where thieves break in and steal; but store up for yourselves treasures in heaven, where neither moth nor rust consumes and where thieves do not break in and steal. Matthew 6:19-20*

Envy – Wanting what someone else has and resenting them for having it. The Catechism of the Catholic Church states "When it wishes grave harm to a neighbor it is a mortal sin."

> *And he said, "It is what comes out of a person that defiles. For it is from within, from the human heart, that evil intentions come: fornication, theft, murder, adultery, avarice, wickedness, deceit, licentiousness, envy, slander, pride, folly. All these evil things come from within, and they defile a person." Mark 7:20-23*

> *"For where your treasure is, there your heart will be also" Matthew 6:21*

Greed – intense and selfish desire for something, especially wealth, power, or food. Beware of those preachers who preach the prosperity gospel and could be leading you into sin as they themselves sin.

> *And he said to them, "Take care! Be on your guard against all kinds of greed; for one's life does not consist in the abundance of possessions." Luke 12:15*

> *Jesus, looking at him, loved him and said, "You lack one thing; go, sell what you own, and give the money to the poor, and you will have treasure in heaven; then come, follow me." When he heard this, he was shocked and went away grieving, for he had many possessions. Mark 10:21-22*

Worldliness – the condition of being concerned with worldly affairs, especially to the neglect of spiritual things. Are we more concerned with wearing the latest fashion, what is happening in entertainment and social media than we are the things of God? Do we conform ourselves to the social norms of modern society or to God's laws?

> *As for what was sown among thorns, this is the one who hears the Word, but the cares of the world and the lure of wealth choke the Word, and it yields nothing. Matthew 13:22*

> *For what will it profit them if they gain the whole world but forfeit their life? Or what will they give in return for their life? Matthew 16:26*

> *Do not deceive yourselves. If you think that you are wise in this age, you should become fools so that you may become wise. For the wisdom of this world is foolishness with God. For it is written, "He catches the wise in their craftiness," 1 Corinthians 3:18-19*

SINNERS' PRAYERS

Jewish Prayer

Please God! I have intentionally sinned, I have sinned out of lust and emotion, and I have sinned unintentionally. I have done [such-and-such] and I regret it, and I am ashamed of my deeds, and I shall never return to such a deed.

Catholic Act of Contrition

O my God, I am heartily sorry for having offended You, and I detest all my sins because of Your just punishments, but most of all because they offend You, my God, Who art all-good and deserving of all my love. I firmly resolve, with the help of Your grace, to sin no more and to avoid the near occasions of sin.

Protestant Sinners' Prayer

Heavenly Father I come before you in prayer asking for the forgiveness of my sins. I confess with my mouth and believe with my heart that Jesus is your Son, and that he died on the Cross at Calvary that I might be forgiven and have Eternal Life in the Kingdom of Heaven. Father, I believe that Jesus rose from the dead and I ask you right now to come into my life and be my personal Lord and Savior. I repent of my sins and will worship you all the days of my life! Because your word is truth, I confess with my mouth that I am born again and cleansed by the blood of Jesus! In Jesus' name. Amen.

Muslim Du'a

Our Lord! Grant us forgiveness and mercy! For You are the best of those who show mercy. Oh my Lord, I have indeed wronged my soul! Our Lord! We have indeed believed. Forgive us our sins and save us from the agony of the Fire. Our Lord! Condemn us not if we forget or fall into error. Our Lord! Lay not on us a burden like that which You did lay on those before us. Our Lord! Lay not on us a burden greater than we have strength to bear. Blot out our sins, and grant us forgiveness. Have mercy on us. You are our Protector. Help us against those who stand against faith.

SUMMARY

When we come to understand what offends God, how should we react? Despair, that there are too many ways to break God's commandments and too many weaknesses and difficulties in our nature to keep them? No, God will help us, through His grace, if we seek Him with a sincere heart.

> *From His fullness we have all received, grace upon grace. The law indeed was given through Moses; grace and truth came through Jesus Christ. John 1:16-17*

> *When the disciples heard this, they were greatly astounded and said, "Then who can be saved?" But Jesus looked at them and said, "For mortals it is impossible, but for God all things are possible." Matthew 19:25-26*

What is important is that we make it our life's mission to obey the commandments as Jesus taught his disciples in the Lord's prayer to submit to the Father's will. After all, He made us and knows what is best for us.

> *Pray then in this way: Our Father in heaven, hallowed be your name. Your kingdom come. Your will be done, on earth as it is in heaven. Give us this day our daily bread. And forgive us our debts, as we also have forgiven our debtors. And do not bring us to the time of trial, but rescue us from the evil one. Matthew 6:9-13*

St Peter reminds us in Acts how important our obedience to God is.

> *But Peter and the apostles answered, "We must obey God rather than any human authority." Acts 5:29*

The Old Testament instructs the descendants of Abraham to do God's will.

*I delight to do your will, O my God; your law is
within my heart. Psalm 40:8*

*The secret things belong to the Lord our God, but the
revealed things belong to us and to our children forever,
to observe all the words of this law.
Deuteronomy 29:29*

In the Quran, Mohamed's followers are exhorted to live a righteous
life.

*All that - its evil is ever, in the sight of your Lord,
detested. Surah Al-Isra 17:39*

In the New Testament, Jesus reminds his disciples to seek God's
kingdom first, to take up our crosses, and enter through the narrow
gate.

*But strive first for the kingdom of God and his
righteousness, and all these things will be given to you
as well. Matthew 6:33*

*Then he said to them all, "If any want to become my
followers, let them deny themselves and take up their
cross daily and follow me." Luke 9:23*

*Enter through the narrow gate; for the gate is wide
and the road is easy that leads to destruction, and
there are many who take it. For the gate is narrow
and the road is hard that leads to life, and there are
few who find it. Matthew 7:13-14*

Will you seek the Kingdom of God first?

Will you take up your cross and follow the Lord?

Will you enter through the narrow gate?

The invitation is there; all you need to do is accept it, submit to it,
and follow it, with God's help.

INDEX

ABOUT THE AUTHOR

Karen Marie Matthews is Executive Director of One Bread Lay Apostolate, a Catholic lay non-profit organization dedicated to evangelizing the gospel as taught by the Catholic Church. The organization is also committed to ecumenism and strives to bring all Christians to greater unity to fulfill Jesus' desire that his disciples be one.

*I have other sheep that do not belong to this fold. I
must bring them also, and they will listen to my voice.
So there will be one flock, one shepherd. John 10:16*

Karen works full-time as a technical writer, runs a part-time souvenir business, and is the author of a children's book entitled "The Legend of Lizard Lick: A North Carolina Folktale." She is a daughter, wife, a mother, and most importantly a child of God.

For free information about the teachings of the Catholic Church,
visit the website of
One Bread Lay Apostolate
www.onebread.us.com

www.ingramcontent.com/pod-product-compliance
Lightning Source LLC
Chambersburg PA
CBHW060611030426
42337CB00018B/3045